Eros & Thanatos

Eros & Thanatos

Sashibhusan Rath

2021

BLACK EAGLE BOOKS

USA address:
7464 Wisdom Lane
Dublin, OH 43016

India address:
E/312, Trident Galaxy, Kalinga Nagar,
Bhubaneswar-751003, Odisha, India

E-mail: info@blackeaglebooks.org
Website: www.blackeaglebooks.org

First International Edition Published by
BLACK EAGLE BOOKS, 2021

EROS & THANATOS
by Sashibhusan Rath

Original Copyright © **Sashibhusan Rath**

All rights reserved. No part of this publication may be reproduced, stored in a retrieval system, or transmitted, in any form or by any means, electronic, mechanical, photocopying, recording or otherwise without the prior permission of the publisher.

Cover Design: **Ritayan**, Frankfurt
Inner drawing: **Rishikesh**, Bengaluru
Interior Design: Ezy's Publication

ISBN- 978-1-64560-226-2 (Paperback)
Library of Congress Control Number: 2021950706

Printed in the United States of America

A thinker fathers a thought and an artist adorns it with beauties of sound, colour and movement. Sigmund Freud, the father of psychoanalytic movement, spawned "Eros" (Greek word for God of Love) and "Thanatos" (Greek word for God of Death) to epitomize the process of creation and the return to the state of nirvana. Eros stand for everything that affords pleasure, activity, movement and expansion. Thanatos denotes a state of inorganic entity. The primary drives of eros and thanatos have become buzz words to depict the expanding universe of all we do and cherish.

However, symbolic words are not birds imprisoned in the nest of theories and concepts. They fly and migrate. With poetic spell of imagination of the Mr.Sashibhusan Rath, the symbols have acquired life qualities. The merging of the physical and psychological is depicted with all its splendour. I feel the poetic lines of "Eros and Thanatos" vibrate when readers inhale the oxygen of love and life in their breathing space. I greatly appreciate Mr. Rath for his efficacy and exploration.

Prof. F.M. Sahoo
Ph.D. (Queen's, Canada)
Visiting Professor, Xavier University
(Former Professor & Head, Centre of
Advanced Study in Psychology,
Utkal University, Bhubaneswar)

Introduction

In Greek mythology, Eros was the Greek god of love and sex. In the Theogony of Hesiod (700 BCE), Eros was a primeval god, son of Chaos (the original primeval emptiness of the universe) but later tradition made him the son of Aphrodite (goddess of sexual love and beauty) by either Zeus (the king of the gods), Ares (god of war and of battle), or Hermes (divine messenger of the gods).

Eros was a god not simply of passion but also of fertility. His brother was Anteros(the god of mutual love) who was sometimes described as his opponent. The chief associates of Eros were Pothos and Himeros (Longing and Desire). Roman counterpart of Eros was Cupid . Eros has the ability to make mortals and gods fall in love by shooting them with his bow and arrow. This would work on both mortals and gods.

Thanatos, in ancient Greek religion and mythology, was the personification of death. Hesiod thought that Thanatos was the son of the Nyx (goddess of the night) and the Erebus (god of darkness). This makes Thanatos dark and negative. His twin brother is Hypnos, the god of sleep. He appeared to humans to carry them off to the underworld when the time allotted to them by the Fates had expired.

It is believed Thanatos to be always nearby Eros. They are brothers. One represents the life and creation and another death and destruction. In Greek mythology, Eros is the god of love, and Thanatos is the god of death, making them opposite of one another. Eros is portrayed as nice, compassionate, loving, and full of life. This is how Eros came to represent the instinct of life. People who are driven by life instincts are often happy, compassionate, and social. Thanatos is associated with violent death and would be called upon by gods who wished to inflict death upon one another. Thanatos often manifested anger, violence, and aggression. These characteristics are portrayed in those who are driven by death instincts.

The story of Eros and Thanatos inspired Sigmund Freud(6/5/1856-23/9/1939) to create a psychological theory that a person's instincts fall into one of two categories: the Eros category or the Thanatos category. Sigmund Freud believed that a person's instincts are driven by life or death, and this profound theory is still studied and considered today. He believed that everyone falls under either of these

Influence of Freud is writ large in my poems, rather I have a life-long fixation with his ideas. My first collection of poems Tributaries bear ample testimony to this. Present collection could have been named as Kama & Yama, Mithuna & Moksha, Love & Death or Mrutyusundari but after contemplation I prefer to retain the Greek words.

Life is a series of poems for me and a part revelation of my life is through these poems. It is unjust on my part to say that each poem is complete by itself, as I have realized that words are not adequate and appropriate enough to express feelings. I have further realized that any kind of ritual may not be always productive as expected and my poems too were not written daily as a ritual.

No collection pleases everybody but I hope this one reaches the general public as well as serious students of poetry (as long as they are not serious all the time). I feel this book will interest everyone with an interest in the erotic and the sublimity of death. I hope, too, the book will readily exhibit its own intrinsic appeal and that it might even exert a seminal influence on younger generations.

Thanks to the renowned publisher Black Eagle Books, Dublin, USA for their keen interest in this book.

■

SYMBOL OF YIN & YANG

This collection has 69 poems. Under Eros 35 and under Thanatos 34. The symbol above also indicates 69.It is a circle made up of black and white swirls in 69 shape each containing miniscule circle of the other. Black is yin, white is yang. Female and male principles. Birth and death. Small circle of opposing colour symbolizes that neither is absolute yet both are complementary, interconnected and interdependent. Together they are in a dynamic flux representing a complex relational symbol. Interestingly on rotation there is interchange ability of the colours 6 and 9 swirl of this ancient Chinese symbol.

∎

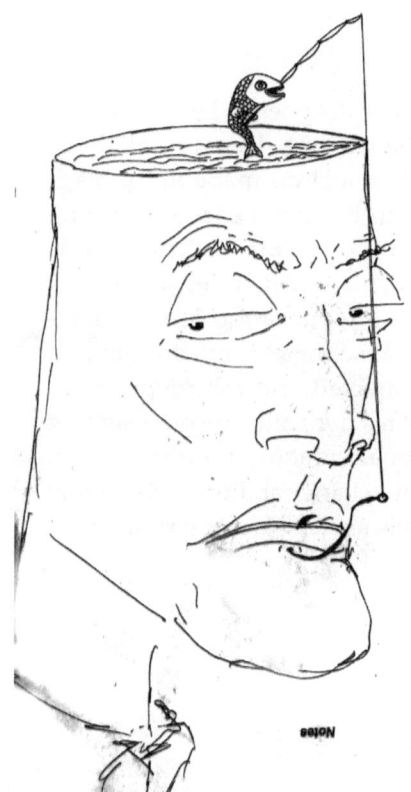

AN ACt OF CREATION
CRISHI

CONTENTS

EROS

Extinct Mothers	15
Haikus For Vatsyayana	17
Recipe	29
Birdy Words	31
Sperm Bank	33
Life And Love	34
Skin Game	35
Night Vision	36
She	37
Containment	39
Honeycomb	40
A Whore	41
Love&Lust	42
Lover	43
Day & Night	44
Menu	46
Copyright	48
No Time	50
Nympho-Trap	51
Beauty	52
Ways Of Nature	53
Confession Of A Prostitute	54
A Vision	56
Love	57
Native Rape	58
Hermaphrodite	59
Yin&Yang	61
Love & Sex	63
Body Text	64
Illusion&Disillusion	65
Chambermaid Of 116	66

Nudity	67
Ban	68
Prostitute	69
Men&Women	70

THANATOS

Cypher Guru	73
To My Bier Carriers	75
The Bicycle	77
Just For A Price	78
Enemies Of Faith	79
Brewing Time	81
Underbelly	83
Writer Munda	85
Approximations	87
Mahabharata Here & Now	89
Quantum Signature	92
Silence	93
Three Liners From Self-Exile	95
Orifice	101
Crime & Punishment	102
Periodicity	104
Earth Of Mortals	105
Visit Ends	107
Setting Sun	108
A Desire I Live With	109
Goodbye	110
Life	111
Gunpont	113
The Last Licence	114
A Wish	115
Sphinx	116
Viscera	117
Mutinies	118
House Arrest	119
End Game	120
Death	121
Spider	122
Now Here , Now Nowhere	123
Last Wish	125

EROS

EXTINCT MOTHERS

Women today refuge to be the seat of creation.
She refuges to be matrix of birth.
Has no desire to be the first teacher.
She condemns and raise slogans against
Defining women as child bearing pouches.
She gives the clarion call to unite
To protest against child bearing.
She wants to spring up
In career and in public life.
She wants to be a copy cat
And likes to catwalk before the hungry onlookers.
She dreams of a world
Full of women without uterus.
She says banning the bra was not enough
Discarding the uterus
Shall lead to total liberation.
Uncomfortable little kicks in the uterus
Are not longer desirable.
Therefore, no offspring please she says.
Instead she wants to be
A marketable product....
To live till she draws others attention.
Once it is gone
She wants to recede into oblivion forever.

Of course, not as a mother
Only as a beautiful woman.
She says what all she believes :
One day the earth will be motherless
Causing the homo sapiens to extinct.

■

HAIKUS FOR VATSYAYANA

As a young man Vatsyayana wrote Kamasutra, the classic treatise on sex describing the objectives, methods and aesthetics. It was not pornography then, nor it is now. Kamasutra shall be in demand so long as love predominates death, so long as mankind survives on the power of sex. Khajuraho with all its erotic sculptures carved on its body complete more than a thousand years of existence and a few haikus are written keeping Vatsyayana in mind. Primarily haikus, are of Japanese origin known for their lucidity, brevity, and meaningfulness.

It is said of a woman that the more is the vocabulary the less is expressed of a woman. An Italian proverb compares a translation to a woman , the more beautiful the translation , the more unfaithful it is(una traduzione e coma, piu e belle piu e falsa). So was my feeling when I transcribed my thoughts to haikus with care. The

Expressions which follow are not exactly haikus but haiku-like, written to mould the imagination of the readers:

●
Why to be faithful
To the other half?
●

For the lonely when it rains
Other's absence is felt.
•
There is no time for making love,
Anytime is the time to love.
•
The newly-wed hide their passion
From the prying eyes of those experienced folk.
•
Passion has the ember of moonlight
Slow, bewitching and never-ending.
•
Her eyes are eager when he has not reached
They look away when he reaches !
•
When she looks at him and he at her
The pollen talcum falls in their eyes, in their heart.
•
When he imagines her, he is bitten by the love-bug
One wonders why such imagination bites !
•
She does not smell of any flower known hitherto
The fragrance of her ambrosia fills him in ecstasy.
•
When young she was innocent and beautiful
Now she is no longer innocent nor naïve.
•
In winter she loves the sunshine spread on her body
In summer the butterfly touching her and flying away.
•
The unlucky pearls are inside the oyster
Only the lucky ones nestle between her breasts.
•

A petty girls breasts are for admiration
Only young hearts dare to look at them.
●
Her pretty face, and her desirable body, her waist
Only make her an appetizer for men.
●
The curves and slopes of her body are exquisite
Even the beholders' gaze slide over them !
●
Her waist and neck have the elements of a peacock,
Breasts of a dove, eyes of a deer.
●
There is magic in her skin, eyes and gait
Like a magician she makes herself wanted and unwanted.
●
When both are in unison she is he, he is she
When they are not, she is she, he is he.
●
When she steals her gaze from him
There is forest fire, her lips brighten with flame.
●
Her body is not of golden hue, as it looks
It is of Egyptian cotton treated with moonlight.
●
When both are in unison for sometime
She realizes what she is, and he what he is.
●
Why men, her body has even seduced gods
Unfailingly over the millennia.
●
Her eyebrows, eyes, nose, lips, cheeks, nipples ,
Navel, closet ,arms, legs, fingers are all invitingly virtuous.
●

She uses her looks, her ornaments,
And hidden arsenals at appropriate time.
●
He is nothing, incomplete , partial
Until his lust is met by her.
●
Decide to be or not to be, to do or not to do,
To be is to enjoy and not to be is to pray.
●
He too enjoys food like her
But nothing is more joyous than sex.
●
When she is indifferent she is unfathomable and poison
She can burn him right there
●
Both of them desire for a longer attachment
But time detaches them for their good.
●
Her face, the pearl and the moon
Define a new equinox accentuating sex.
●
He loves all who are small and beautiful
When he sees her, holds her firmly and makes love.
●
The lily faced , honey lipped, full bosomed women
Have teased the horny maleness at all times.
●
Who says there is a coiled snake in her ?
Who says the latent snake releases honey and no poison?
●
When her passion is aroused time is stilled
He makes his way into her to live and let her live.
●

When her passion is aroused
Nothing can obstruct her from compulsive coition.
•
Her belly button hole is a mute witness
To the merger of time and distance between him and her.
•
When they are lost in the act of love
They are made for each other and none else.
•
She has enjoyed her moments with him and he with her
How can they separate severing all memories ?
•
He feels her to be uniquely beautiful hitherto unknown
She is proud of her own beauty but more proud of him.
•
She combines the beauty, the sin, the sex and the virtue
She offers her inviting body.
•
Once upon a time only the perfume, the music
Were so inviting to have sex, but not now.
•
Her slender waist and smooth thighs
Are as hungry as the canyon
•
One upon the other
Neither said anything.
•
When she kisses him in quick succession
She demonstrates the agility of a snake.
•
Half moon is only her face
Full moon is she in her totality.
•

When the fire of love erupts in her
She becomes uncontrollable.

•

She enjoys pain in pleasure
She enjoys sex with bruises.

•

Her body is a vast empire
Nevertheless she takes care of the minutest

•

When she lifts her arms and closes her eyes
Her breasts look at the sky in vain.

•

The passionate embrace of her breasts
Never leaves any strain on his hairy chest.

•

When both are entangled physically and emotionally
Nothing remains to be explained between him and her.

•

Also when everybody sleeps all around
They make love silently, as if secretly !

•

Amidst the noise of passing trains near their habitat
Their laughter is lost in such noise when they indulge in sex.

•

Her face, her wet lips, her breasts and the lascivious triangle
Constitute nothing but petals of the same fragrant flower.

•

Breasts are crushed and crushed again
But they revive to the initial glory like a phoenix.

•

She was fragrant, she said he too was fragrant
Both grabbed each other and lost in ambrosia.

•

She said she loved the big snake
Hissing and licking her dark and deep interiors.
●
So many petals blossom on her body
When she lies hot on him.
●
After making love she too walks naked
But she looks shy and her body looks so lovely.
●
When they hold each other in tight embrace
Something melts somewhere, deep within.
●
When the eyes speak, lips quiver, bodies tremble
It is time for coition, no excuses from either him or her.
●
Her eyes are closed but she is wide awake within
When he enters her, the young bride plays her own game.
●
The bodice ,the petticoat, the ornaments are all meaningless;
When she removes everything from her body at primetime.
●
Often she wants him to untie her attire
But he does not understand and prefers to enter her.
●
In her flight of imagination she often thinks
Let her bodice snap by her swollen breasts.
●
When they ride each other doing sex
They forgive each other without any pretence.
●
Excessive love have wasted her breasts
Her nipples do not look up any longer.
●

As a naïve young bride she is afraid and repents
Seeing the evidence on her body and bed.

•

When she is playful and has enjoyed every move
She leaves no evidence on bed whatsoever.

•

Secret bruises on her breasts and hips
Can only be read by her when she looks at them.

•

Her hips and breasts are abundant;
Of what use are they , if not skillfully handled by him ?

•

She is no longer a fearful young bride
She desires him more and more for sex.

•

Yesterday she was hiding her breasts with her palms
Today she is not hideous, her body closet is wide open.

•

There is osmosis between them while in coition
He has her fragrance, she has his odour.

•

Her palms yearns for hardness, for support
His palms strive for softness to live and let live.

•

Staring at the breasts and the cleavage
Is a primordial activity neither wrong nor sinful.

•

To have sex on horse's back or an elephant's
Both enjoy such wild imagination.

•

When he rests his palm on the groove between her thighs
Skillfully her fingers pierce into his hips.

•

She is bruised ,love-marks all over her body
She has enjoyed sex yet wants it again.

•

When her body is soft after her menstruation ceases
When her lips are wet she smiles at him bewitchingly.

•

She released all fasteners and garments
And offered herself to him wanting a treat.

•

When she desires and he wills to act
She seeks a kiss on her forehead with her eyes closed.

•

The open secret between her lily white thighs
Entices him to operate.

•

She enjoys the marks of his nails when he does it
Later she rediscovers and recreates in her imagination.

•

She doesn't cover her breasts nor her open-secret
She is no longer innocent and shy of sex.

•

She is no longer shy, nor feels secretive
She says let the neighbours know our act.

•

Her naked body is a feast for the eyes
Her body is full, complete and attractive.

•

She is born intelligent, doesn't need lessons
She guides him for her own enjoyment.

•

Her breasts are magic mountains
Slopes awaiting eagerly for skillful mountaineers.

•

She is thirsty, hungry and vacant
She quenches herself mating with him lustfully.
•
When he prays does he really forget her ?
When he mounts her does he really forget prayer?
•
When they are eager for sex and doing the foreplay
Musk emanates from him, flowery fragrance from her.
•
Between them sex is the greatest common denominator
And she loves ornaments, he loves heady fragrance.
•
Both are clever, intelligent and very active on bed
He handles large-breasted women , she the muscular men.
•
Sweet nothing words, foreplay, blushing shame
Mack anger are all trivialities before sex.
•
The feel of her breasts , smell of her tresses switches him on
This muscular arm and flat chest make her ecstatic.
•
Her thrusting hips and upward looking breasts
Are made for his strong chest and muscular fingers.
•
Her naturally fragrant body attracts the butterflies
And he takes a shortcut to her virgin forest for merry making.
•
Initially she says no, but then opens herself at ease
He plays, he grabs and she enjoys the game plentifully.
•
After the sex she wants him again
Then he is playful again and she is considerate.
•

When she desires, she becomes wild and irresistible
When he desires, she only can quench his desire.
•
Above the msl (mean sex level) rises the dome of desire
His minaret too trembles to penetrate her.
•
The thin line of wandering hair down her navel
Is only a trail of smoke implying a fire underneath.
•
After making love again and again
She looks at him and he at her, lying side by side.
•
Love and lust overwhelm him into frenzied despair
He plays on her body, with her body, only to her delight.
•
When he stands stark naked before her like a beast unleashed
She turns ecstatic and closes her eyes in shame.
•
They made love in so many ways
Goose-pimples and colours writ large on their bodies.
•
Whenever she desires him, she covers her breast with her palms
Once she releases her palms, swiftly she hides her secret triangle.
•
Her heavy fully grown breasts and fatless thighs
Have made him mad to do sexual calisthenics.
•
Her navel is deep, eyes swift, heavy breasts appear unmanageable
When he sees at her narrow waist desire to indulge in quick sex.
•
Her breasts are domes of pleasure, her hips ambrosia
He loves her vigorously to her delight.
•

Unmanageable breasts make her lean forward
Enticing him to grab and manage them.

●

She protests not when he grabs her breasts and buttocks
And then occupies the mound between her thighs.

●

Seeing the young, sexy and desiring woman
The old man recharges his imagination to keep him alive.

●

Love and sex transcends time and age
Who does not want sex?

■

RECIPE

Recipe of war and war mongers
Recipe of victorious and vanquished
Are different from others.
To preserve power war continues
Barracks and brothels get closer
Comfort women and cheer girls
Are the debris of war
Served attractively today.
Who knows?
Next hot spot for us will be sex
Available in assembly line
Customers moving in queue
Getting their hunger satiated.
Even rape will be absorbed
With lighter punishment
When woman gets objectified.
They say
The male gaze dictates
The use of women's bodies.
The glamorous women
Is for consumption
By pent-up males.
The pin-up glamorous women
On the barber's plank walls
Or on the glossy cover pages

Are eye tonics.
They say
It is a never-ending quest
For perfection
In an imperfect world
Both for females and males.
And it goes on.

BIRDY WORDS

From nowhere the words come
And perch on the mind's foliage.
Like birds rarely they settle
To make a nest.
Like birds
Words too are always on the move.
They prefer to fly away
To an unknown space
May be from where they had come.

SPERM BANK

Mediocre people are mushrooming
Here there
All over the globe.
Mothers are getting extinct
No woman wants to be.
In vitro, surrogate mothers
Are in plenty
Choice is with the women
To go for the best.
She wants the offspring
Of the best sperm.
Sperm banks have become a reality.
Legendary men and women
Can be born again.
Nothing divine
Nothing meteoric.
Anytime anywhere
A sperm can be coalesced
With an ovum
Fertilized conveniently
Producing a scientist
A nobel laureate, a jazz singer
Or a statesman !
Males will be sperm producers
And females

The producers of quality babies.
Pregnancy will only be mental
That's too for poets, architects, artists
Who shall conceive and create.
Pregnancy will no longer be physical
For women
No blues, no pains.

LIFE AND LOVE

Life is not love.
Love is not life.
Love is living every moment
Against the drudgery of life.
Living for others is love indeed,
Dying for others is love indeed.
Life without love is no life.
Where there is no life
There is no love.
Life is colourful, so is love.
Life has its pains, so is love.
Life ends, love too ends.
From nature life has emerged,
From life love has emerged.
Love gives life a meaning,
Life becomes meaningful to live.

SKIN GAME

Mirror, mirror on the wall
Who's the fairest of us all ?
Fairness for face
Fairness for underarms
Fairness for private parts
Consumer labels all around.
Nothing wrong in being fair
So long you dare
To look young and attractive
For your opposite sex.
After all it is all a game
A skin game, a fair game !
Fairness matters
Whether it is skin or otherwise.
And now there is competiotion
For immortality on glossy papers.
Women go topless
And pose nude for charity……..
May be for cosmetic testing,
May be for protection of animals,
Or for landmines, breast cancer.
Of course, it is always good
To shed all clothes
For a noble cause.

NIGHT VISION

When the late night flight to Kolkata
Was in landing mode in midnight
Looking down through the window
An apparition appeared to me :
A vast black bare bosomed
Woman shape
With her eyes burning like brazier
Looking at the star-studded sky
Lying flat on land
With a fire burning on her palm.
City lighting golden and silver
Looked like her ornaments.
As the aircraft was heading
Like a black eagle,
Slowly the shape disappeared
To nowhere,
From where she appeared.
But I felt she was still there
Permeated everywhere.
She has left an indelible imprint
In my mind forever...
Something interesting and mysterious
To cherish...

SHE

For her the ultimate masculinity
Is either a dog, a bull or an elephant.
Her secret intoxicating phrases
Are only understood by her lover.
The flameless fire urns in him
For consummating her, glorifying her.
His combustion within
And the expressed love
Is a tribute to her body beautiful.
There is a magic in her voice,
There is hunger between her lips
And a pair of doves of rare breed
Waiting for a caress on her bosom.
When she curses or praises someone
It is only to linger the embrace.
Every thirst in her lips entices
For a warm onslaught but
Never quenched,
A never ending
Painless way to salvation.
She knows after occupying her house
And drinking her choicest bevearage
His thirst is not quenched,
As he drinks more and more
Never tired of bouts of pleasure.

She understands well
When she speaks about exploding stars
Or when he speaks about glory of creation

■

CONTAINMENT

The love between lovers die
With their extinction.
Memories of embrace, the fire,
And all those callisthenics
Get extinguished,
As soon as the lovers
Become traceless
On this mundane earth.
Lovers are not immortal,
Unless they reach the precipice
Of their love sanguine.
Love is blind forever,
Whether active or inert,
Love kills and knows not
Whom it wounds more.
It is only a killing field
Where the lovers perform
Their callisthenics,
Whether in private or in public.
Love is a poison so sweet
And it kills so slowly
Before the lovers are aware.
Contentment is what they want
More than the poisonous containment.

HONEYCOMB

There is a drop of poison.
Its presence makes her body
Curvaceous and intoxicating.
The blood-red poison reflects
On her lips and bosom.
She is a blending of
Wine red and white.
Her body is a flower vase
Full of wine,
Soft, supple and charming too.
Making love to her means
Entering into a
Hidden treasure trove
Unfathomable and revealing.
She hides a honeycomb,
And when honey overflows
None can go against her desire
To love and be loved.
When the honey is intoxicating
It is poisonous
But more desirable.
Days pass with wine,
Honey and poison...
And that is also life,
Digging into an infinite well
Full of carnal viscosity,
Of heaven and hell coexisting.

A WHORE

When the rich old man
Started crawling like a predator
On her voluptuous body,
It was frustrating for her
And she was thinking
For her next customer.
The predator beast tried
To crush her to the bones
But failed...
It all ended,
As a tragic end for him
And a farce for her.
Ironically he was satisfied
With what he did to her,
And whatever little pleasure
Was hesitantly offered by her.
The next customer
Was younger to her,
And his game of sex
Was real fun for her,
And she resisted
Only to be overpowered
By the muscular young customer.
They had grapes
Between vigorous bouts of sex.

■

LOVE & LUST

Touch during sex
Is less of love more of lust.
Unless it is an onslaught
It is no sex.
Unless there are love bites,
Nail bruises at buttocks,
It is no sex.
Sex has now become more beastly
Than what the beasts do.
Excess lust of man
Sees the woman
Only as a fertile delta
Ever-ready for tilling.
Violent sex leaves its marks
Indelible and memorable.
All sex begins
With non-violence,
But once the mutually satisfying
Onslaught starts,
There is lots of fire and fury
Ending in a bloodless coup
Encroaching silently
Into the area of jurisprudence.
Total non-violent sex
Is a myth perhaps.

LOVER

A lover becoming a wanderer
Is not uncommon.
A lover waiting for a glimpse
Of his beloved for hours
Is not uncommon.
A lover squandering everything
For her sake, for her pleasure
Is not uncommon.
But that's all Platonic.
Being a woman she was fond of
Wealthy, ornaments
Apparels and gifts
But above everything else was
Her insatiable desire for sex.
It is however not uncommon.
Today lovers are slaves of mobile,
Busy in hasty dating,
Frequent sex with protective sheaths
With changing partners
Is not uncommon.
Everything is fun,
Love in vehicle, in rented suite,
Mutually convenient
Medical termination
Of accidental pregnancies
Is the in thing. ■

DAY & NIGHT

The lovers are ready
To ride each other on bed
As per their need.
They know anytime is love time,
That's what they learnt
From the birds and bulls.
She avoids daylight's brutal glare,
And defers sex till night,
When she throws away
Her veil of modesty in gay abandon.
He however prefers another round
At wee hours before daybreak.
In early years she enjoyed sex
With her eyes closed,
And he had his attires on his body.
They too evolved to naked sex
With their eyes wide open
Performing successfully
Prolonged coitus(sukha mithuna)
Ending in orgasm(ashoka ananda).
Sex is not shameless in radiant light
Sex is not blind in pitch darkness.
When the places of worship
Are locked indefinitely
For reasons whatsoever

Or there is a war at the borders,
Eros* the God of sex rules always.
Sex is the life force
That keeps the wheel of life moving.

*Eros is the son of Aphrodite and Ares(Chaos).
Fully grown adult male Greek God of love
and sex, with wings. Roman counterpart of
Eros is Cupid.

MENU

On a lonely terrace
She bared her body
Her nipples were pointed to the moon.
It was a full moon night
And her marble white body
Was looking more beautiful
With the moon shine spreading all over.
She too was delighted
Seeing her own body beautiful.
She was waiting for her lover to come,
And the waiting was appetizing for her.
Intermittently she gently massaged
Her fully grown breasts and the abdomen.
She was stark naked,
But not ashamed of the moon at all.
For the lover she was a delicious recipe,
To be enjoyed under romantic moonlight.
On arrival the lover was intensely excited
And was transfixed
On her pinnacle of nipples.
His eyes were searching for the rose bud,
With an innate desire to touch.
The atmosphere was like a perfumed garden
And a mortal Venus was ready
For coitus with her body concoction.

He felt intoxicated with her breathy embrace.
He tilled into her honeyed patch of flesh
And she enjoyed the invading healthy flesh
As she was waiting so long for
Such a deep rooted penetration.
She guided him into her untouched depths
For the heightened resonance of pleasure.

COPYRIGHT

Her lascivious gait and walk
Made her the most wanted woman
And a beauty queen
In the college corridors.
Everybody wanted to see her,
She never looked at anybody
But exuded beauty and body odour
For the passers by to look back.
Her vanity was in full blossom,
Marble white skin, dovelike bosom,
And throne-like thighs
Enriched her pendulous motion.
But alas!
A conservative marriage
To a high circle officer
Was a disgrace to the beauty queen
As he failed to unleash
The beast from his cage.
It all ended in a separation
And she went abroad forever
For a more permissive life
Fulfilling all her needs and hunger.
She still feels none can copy her.

She lives with a notion
That she has the copyright
Of whatever she holds in her.
She is perhaps a mirror image of
Gender reversed Narcissus.

■

NO TIME

These days lovers have no time in hand
Nobody wants to suffer the pains of passion,
Nobody understands
The behind every kiss.
They know not
That the choice of love combines
The best and the worst without restraint.
Lovers want to delay the nights
But love
Restraints the ongoing smelting.
They know not
That when love is harsh
It separates them effortlessly,
Exposes their weaknesses
Before they realise privately.
Love only teaches them
Restraint, caution and cure.
Love only reminds the lustful touches,
Nefarious pleasures, ecstasy
And the carnal feast of sex.

NYMPHO-TRAP

Cheek to cheek
She murmured a sweet word of love,
And successfully extracted a promise
From me at that moment.
In that brief perfumed interlude
Her pearl earring fell on my feet.
I wondered whether it was intentional.
I knew her husband was my classmate,
I also knew she was a nymphomaniac,
Her appetite for sex often unbridled.
Her beneficiaries never called her
A whore, a slut or a harlot,
She was just a charming woman
In the eyes of the beholder.
On the promised day
I returned her earring,
She played with it for a while
And she expressed her gratitude
With a blissful act of sex with me,
Without any hesitations.

BEAUTY

Beauty is a conundrum in itself
It is difficult to pinpoint where it is.
Beauty is not on the surface skin
Nor it is shin deep.
May be it is in the eyes of the beholder.
Let the truth of beauty be behind the veil.
Who knows unveiling may reveal poison.
Beauty is not body
Never revealed through kneading
Neither digging nor dissection helps
May be it lives in the mind.
Perhaps it is expressed through
Art, literature, painting and architecture.
Beauty reveals itself from nowhere,
Perseverance through the act of creativity
Fructifies the labour of love.
Sometimes a beautiful work
Hides an untold romance
Between the art and the artist.
The maker exists in his own makings,
Plagiarists ultimately perish
Under the blade of time.
They have no place
In a world of beauty, love and art .

WAYS OF NATURE

Let us understand,
How beautifully water flows,
And the blood in the body too.
Stars and galaxies move in the cosmos
So are the atoms in us.
Let us understand how beautifully
Nature follows her course
Created by herself,
And neither there are collisions
Nor any accidents.
Let us understand
How beautifully the nature
Invents and discovers continually.
And there are never ending
Genus and species
Enriching the creation all the time.
We only discover laws, disciplines
And characteristic patterns in nature
As a part of our creative whims
And take credits and receive awards !

CONFESSION OF A PROSTITUTE

"I was barely eleven
When I was raped unknowingly,
Then repeatedly raped on the fields..
And therefore schooling didn't last long.
Every month ,
The witch mother at the end of the village
Washed my uterus
Injecting vegetable poison and water.
She knew the local rapists
But remained silent
As they had threatened to murder her.
Thereafter I have only been interested
More in men and their ways
Of rough handling of my body.
I always craved
For the violence of sex
Although it used to be
Obnoxious and painful.
But there was no scope for
Resistance or revolt.
I waited for their arrival
And listened their lewd bargain.

But they went for the flesh
Sold by the lowest bidder.
I therefore revolt within
Against all women.
My hidden part may distract me
But attract the males.
Men are still attracted towards me
And I have learnt how to
Make a full-grown man
Beg for more and more sex from me.
Some were fond of
My full breast spilling out
Of white cotton bras.
And days pass making way
For the new customers."

■

A VISION

That primordial intimacy
In the Garden of Eden
Was only an utopian callisthenics.
There was flesh, groan.
Hissing and full-some curiosity
In broad daylight.
That was the only truth,
No corruption, no guilt of sin,
No error , no repentance
Of any syndrome.
Innocence of flesh,
Attraction of naked body-beautiful
Ruled supreme
When the male and female
Were condemned
And left alone in utter privacy
For the progeny to flourish
As a matter of never-ending fun
A game of love and hate..

LOVE

Love was already there
Within us in the gene.
Love was never invented,
It was an ancient discovery.
Love rules supreme,
In an artifact of another dimension,
Let us not save ourselves,
Lat us save our species.
If we don't we shall perish,
No trace of mankind in timeline
Love upholds life against death,
Love is the elixir existence.
Loving unconditionally,
Returns with amazing colours .
There is none devoid of love
As there is none of devoid of heart.

NATIVE RAPE

She resisted as much as she can
But finally surrendered
To the onslaught of five men
Who overpowered her
Pounced on her,
Like hungry cannibals,
Crusting biting into her flesh
As if she was delicious recipe.
They went on raping her
Not knowing she was already dead.
yet their hunger was not satiated,
Until she was abandoned,
Beyond the limits of identity.
Her body was smeared with her own blood
The victorious five, looking back
Were laughing to glory,
Talking aloud top themselves
That lions only catch and eat their prey.
They are always present
 In the cesspool of society,
None can penetrate into
The bottle friendship
And the illicit flesh hunters!
 In the makeshift thesis of divinity
Devil has to live and thrive
As an anti-thesis. ■

HERMAPHRODITE

Human being.
A psychosomatic animal,
Like an earthworm
It also changes its sex
From male to female
And female to male !
When finale she is purgatory
A mature being
Who receives only.
Whenever male
He turns into an operator,
Without any repentance
For all his deeds and misdeeds,
Human being
Once declared spineless
Metaphorically becomes hermaphroditic
Like many other invertebrates -
There is no divinity,
No mystery,
There's nothing extraordinary
In this species of
Homo sapiens
Available in plenty
In bureaucracy, in politics,
In shady areas of corruption,

Trade and commerce.
Long live invertebrate humans !
Long live their ways
Let them mushroom
Till they turn immortals.

YANG & YIN

Yang is masculinity
It is the sun and the sky,
He is the leveller
He gyrates on wet earth
Vigorous and cyclonic.

Everything then subsides
With the debris littered around.
The vigour, the strength
The force, the tempest
All get lost in time.

Yin is feminine
Without her the game is incomplete.
She only gives in to the Yang.
Nothing wrong in their cycle
Yin and Yang coexist.

Like the sunshine and shade
They come and go.
Like happiness and sorrow
One follows the other.
Yang recedes making Yin appear.

After the destruction
There is creation.
It is fragrant everywhere
The butterflies flicker around
Birds chirp in gay abandon.

A new dawn ushers
Mankind absorbs a mayhem.
Love sustains deadly injuries
Children play freely
Birds fly from nowhere to nowhere

Yin is within me
Yang too.
Like the phases of the moon.
Both interplay all the time
They are inseparable continuum.

LOVE & SEX

Urge has two poles
Love and sex.
Urge flourishes
Through these bipolarity.

To be together is love
To touch each other is sex.
Sublimation is love
Penetration is sex.

Love is beyond the eye
Sex is beyond the lips
Love emanates
Sex dissipates.

Love conquers death
Sex conquers time
Love is life
Sex gives life.

Love disappoints
Sex too disappoints,
In the long run perhaps
Love transcends sex.

BODY TEXT

Like a new text
Her body too was read by me.
Those days she was new
Like a new text.

Her body text
Was both within her body
And also on the tips
Of her body surface.

Her body didn't need fabric
Her skin itself was enough.
A rich fabric
Unique by itself.

Her body text
Had a texture of its own
Shinning and soft
Beauty exposed and skin-deep.

ILLUSION & DISILLUSION

She is beautifully fair
She is curvaceous and charming too.
Her eyes are deeply penetrating.
From her translucent attire
She looks irresistibly soft.
Her frontage looks malleable,
My love to her is illusory.

When I look at her back
Her curves are dumb
Only expressionless flesh.
Neither she exposes her back
Nor she has seen herself.
I am disillusioned
But still I love her.

■

CHAMBER MAID OF 116

She called me with esteem
It was a call loaded with passion.
Her big eyes, wide mouth
And revealed fair skin
From her choicest clothes
Invited me to be naughty.
It was an impure wave of life
Full of exotic smell.
She was unmistakably successful
In seducing me
With her titillating words
And her inviting offerings
Writ large on her face and bosom.
St. Valentine's day
Played its own mischief.
A day memorable
For both of us.
Today she is free
Like a humming bird.
Our petals of love vanished in space.

NUDITY

When she is nude invitingly
Her body itself
Is a multi-activity pilgrimage.
Throw away your inhibitions
Keep your culture and preaching
At her doorstep.
Throw away your attire of prejudices
And share the prime time
Drinking the elixir of existence.
Reposition values
Redefine softness
Look beyond the traditions.
The labour is never lost
Moksha is here
Moksha is here
Nowhere else.
It is a juxtaposition
Between the self and beyond.

BAN

All are free to do or whatever they feel.
There is no need to ban.
Banning the books
Banning the bra
Have gone into history.
Today phone and porn
Have become synonyms.
On the small screen.
Of a mobile
Menu served is delicious.
Pornographic films,
Sexy voice to interact
Door delivery of undergarments
Condoms and cosmetics,
Are all commodities.
Demand it, you get it.
Anything, anywhere
Everything can be available
At your very doorsteps !
Ban the word 'ban'
From dictionary.

It is a free, free world.
No chains, no world restrictions
No license, no limits.
It is new world
Banning the ban every moment.

PROSTITUTES

The beauty of the prostitute too
Lies in the eyes of beholder.
This spring they have painted
Their faces to look younger.
Prostitutes are objectified
Manhandled by police & men.
Male prostitutes are gigolos
Women customers
Are too possessive of them
Secretly make them captive.

This spring all look beautiful
All look so young
None can decipher their age.
That is the beauty
Behind all attractions
Of flesh and of mind.

Prostitutes male or female
Are raped
And abandoned to their fate,
Never killed.
But women are raped
And killed to liquidate a witness,
To wipe out evidence.

MEN & WOMEN.

Not all women
Are equally attractive
To all men, all the time.
Not all but some women
Are strongly attractive
For some men.
Women's whole body
From tip to toe
Has always remained
A soft being for men.
Some say,
Women are from Venus
And men from Mars,
Others say,
Women can't read maps
Men can't listen for long.
Women can contain men
Men can't contain women.
Men can dance,
Can play the role of women.
But they are different
Different in many ways
Good for nature
Good for themselves.
They are equal now,
Yet unequal.

THANATOS

CYPHER GURU

He is not a cyber guru.
He is a cypher.
Yet he has followers
Blind followers.
Always ready for him
Even to fall into the abyss,
Whenever there is incoherence,
Vacant looks, tongue-slips,
The followers glorify him saying
He is immersed in divine ecstasy.
 But the fact remains
There is nothing in his mind
His thinking is erratic.
Whenever the sycophants persuade
He speaks on love, life, learning
Lesbianism, Luther, La Vegas.
Then jumps to black hole,
Relativity, chaos, isms,
Prisms, self, souls,
Life after death, universe.
Followers prostrate
And Seek blessings
Cypher gurus gives
With an unchanging smile on his face.
For self renewal

He visits facial parlour
Takes rapid spoken English course
From a divorcee.
Cypher guru is in demand
By both young and old
By those whose soul is impaired
For reasons unknown.

■

MY BIER CARRIERS

Yes I have intimated
A dozen of my well wishers.
To carry my bier
Four at a time.
Whenever anyone feels fatigue
May transfer my dead body load to others.
No sound, no utterances
Only a hurried walk shall guide.
After the formalities
They shall not return unpaid.
I have drawn out
A micro-plan for execution.
Hearing all these they were tearful
But the show has to end.
Yes, some of my friends humbly
Turned down my request.
They gave excuses for
Their inability to carry my bier.
After all, they too are my friends!
Till my end they shall be my friends !
I shall continue to treat them so.
My bier carriers shall not return
With drawn faces.

My kith and kin shall not mourn
Nor shall feast.
I have nothing to give my family,
Only a word of gratitude in advance ,
For my bier carriers.

■

THE BICYCLE

Whether god exists or not,
Which ism is true which is not,
Who is blessed godman and who is nmot
Matters not at all.
The cycle of day and night
The cycle of birth and death
The cycle of creation and destruction
Shall go on for ever.
Apparently real is what we see
Is the cycle of nature
That everything flows from nowhere
To nowhere forever.
But then
There is nothing real or unreal
Everything is in a flux
Appearing as cyclic and acyclic.

■

JUST FOR A PRICE

Just for a price
Anything can be done anywhere.
For a mere price
Explode a bomb to kill
School going innocent children.
Rapist cares not for age
As system frees the rapist not the victim.
Innocence is butchered always
In trains, in court, in commotion.
Women are tortured and highlighted
On Women's Day itself .
High resolution photo is published
Showing the last saliva of starvation.
Girl child foetus is taken away by dog
Abandoned under culvert in broad daylight.
Issueless customers choose the healthy orphan
To adopt but none knows
 What happened next.
Food and flesh have lost their purity
Adulterated for commercial purposes.
We have lost our ethics
We have lost our conscience for a price.
We have lost our cherished freedom
For a mere price.

ENEMIES OF FAITH

From a faith
Well founded or unfounded
He derives sustenance
Of his soul, of his existence.
His father too upheld a faith
Lived for it and died
Never repenting
For what he believed.
Today
Every fifth man
Is an enemy of faith
Trying to demean foundation.
Eradicating the enemies of faith
Is more important
Than the eradication of polio
And of course the mosquitoes.
Let us not forget the fundamentals
On which faith lives on---
Love, trust, compassion, sacrifice
Honesty, truth and tolerance.
Enemies of faith
Have entered deep into the forest
For faith safari
For ethnic conflict.

Beware of the enemies of faith
They are dogs fighting for bones
They are selfish and unethical
Killing others for their own survival.

BREWING TIME

August 15,1947 midnight children
Have all become 66 in 2013.
They all failed to
Make any visible impact.
Millennium dawned
All those born are teens now.
2001 to 2013
Is a short and insignificant
Stride for them.
Can they really face the bad times
Growing around them ?
Frequent shooting at country border,
Beheaded soldiers,
Instability of regional political
Parties within the country,
Rape,ransom
Price hike of water, food , medicines, fuel
...And the list goes on.
Here the poor sells off
His wife and daughter
For a soiled currency note.
Cases go from hundreds to thousands
On every corridor of court.
A spark of revolt
May lead to revolution

But can it be resisted ?
It is brewing time now
Favouring a civil war.
Can the senile leaders
And unfocussed teens
Save India
From the natural brewing
Into a possible civil war ?

∎

UNDERBELLY

Something has gone wrong at
Underbelly.
The cancer suspected
Has spread from the
Urban underbelly to the
Rural underbelly of India.
Rape, ransom, blackmail
Have become the hallmark
Of my country India
Which I have admired
All through my life.
Bad blood is spreading
Like tsunami
Engulfing my own family.
Anything may happen
Anytime, here anywhere
In front of me, behind me.
I am a helpless citizen
Of a tired and old India
Which I cherished
For the values it stood for
When I was young.
Free India then was also young
And I was younger.

Today I can't see her
Tarnished face
But sure enough I can do
Something for her revival
Of charm & charisma

■

WRITER MUNDA

Writer for him was that invisible man
Who fills newspapers daily
With the woes and agonies of his fellow men
Of Karampada, a remote tribal habitat
In the dense Saranda forest
Spreading across Orissa-Jharkhand border.
That unknown tribal father
Wanted his son to be a writer.
The day an elephant delivered an offspring
He named his son Writer Munda.
The child grew to read in the village school
Daily walking alone through dense sal forest,
Rabbits, young cheetahs, rodents
Often looking at him and crossing his path.
As a youth he was an introvert thinking soul
Nurtured carefully in the womb of nature.
He was upright, truthful, not afraid of anybody,
But he was caught by the jungle police.
Before knowing what really happened
He was in the dingy hazat.
Lots of hot light, cameras focused on him
Identified as a terror, cause of bloody crimes.
Writer Munda languished in a jail of
Sundergarh.
Years passed
And he was released as innocent.

But he found nothing in the jungle
His dear ones, the shady trees, his parents
His loving hamlet all have perished.
Like the fallen sal leaves
Unknown, insignificant.
Writer Munda has assimilated time and space
Through torture and loneliness.
The test of fire has steeled him.
He is 21 in 2012
He is roaming free in the vast jungle of Saranda
Never putting a price-tag on his heart and soul
But will the Writer Munda
Will write anything ever?

APPROXIMATIONS

Approximation is no precision.
Approximation is no certainty.
Nothing can be expressed precisely
As uncertainty is the hallmark
Of the ways of nature.
Fleeting ideas, inadequate words
The flux of space and time
Dawn and dusk
Are approximations.
Gazing into the microcosm
Or into the far off macrocosm,
May it be the quantum or cosmos
May it be the ultimate or otherwise
Are only approximations.
Approximation contains the opposites
The existent and the non-existent
Being present or otherwise
Ignorance and knowledge.
In a pulsating universe
Which are there, are not there
As creation and annihilation
Occur every moment.

In transient existence
Nothing is tangible
Except approximations
Only to satisfy the inquisitive.
Ever-changing approximations
Only hint at the ways of nature.
■

MAHABHARATA HERE & NOW

Every moment
Even this fleeting moment
Enacts Mahabharata once again !
A moment's happening
When looked into deeply
Is Mahabharata.
But everyone can't look into
As Dhritarashtra must exist,
And Gandhari too.
Look......
At this moment
Somewhere a Duryodhan
Modern and suit clad
Is sinking deep into
A self-made river of blood !
And there.....
On the pedestrian zebra
A woman is de-robed
Inside a car.
And look.....
At that bright Abhimanyu
Talented, young and creative
So much wanted for the new world.

But see
How he is getting bruised by the elders
By the leaders of men
Who never want
Abhimanyus to grow.
Lest he may snatch away
Their power and glory.
They kill him young.
Brave looking statues are erected
At street corners, schools
In memory of Abhimanyu.
Look......
How the moment stills
When a helpless Draupadi
Is not rescued by Krishna
And instead
Raped and gang raped
Every moment mercilessly.
FIRs are lodged
Without any consequences.
Time has stilled for that Draupadi
Who shall rinse her molested braid
With the blood of those who
Outraged of her modesty.
Padavas were few
Kauravas were many.
Today social workers are few
Politicians are many.
In this ever present Mahabharata
Pandavas lose today
And Kauravas win.
The vital few who matter
And are needed by society

Are burnt alive
Are crushed by the machine
Of administration.
The unended quest
Of Amnesty International
Continues for ever
The trivial many, the mediocre
Laugh to glory for their victory
Over others.
You who read this poem is Arjuna,
A desperate Partha
Searching for self-hood
Always in doubt
A questioning being.
And the Charioteer(sarathi)
Is conspicuously absent
In this intense moment.
All the shades of characters
Appear to grow and perish
In the ever transient moment.
Nobody knows
What survives at the end.
Some say truth lasts
Others say it is only the falsehood
That survives to be visible
So distinctly resplendent
On the face of time.

■

QUANTUM SIGNATURE

Quantum signature is
Omnipresent, omnipotent
And omniscient.
It is a signature
Imbedded in everything
Known and unknown to men.
Signature has no beginning
No end and no dimension
Yet it grows from nowhere to nowhere.
It exists yet exists not
In the DNA ,in the dark matter,
In life and in death.
The signature defines being
And nothingness too,
Manifesting in the grand design
As creation, preservation & annihilation.
Wishful self-organizing quantum signature
Exhales creating stars and galaxies
Inhales into the black-holes.
Unpredictable meteor trail
On wintry night sky
Reminds a signature without any trace…..

SILENCE

I have been silent
Intolerably silent for others.
I have preferred silence
Pervading my being, my existence.
As a bystander
I have seen decades passing by
Burdened with events
Both shameful and praiseworthy.
I know if I open my mouth
My words will set fire
In the hearts of people
Its smoke will pollute
The un-ignited minds of children.
The youth shall come to roads
To protests, demonstrate, resist
As violent rebels
Never bothering about death.
From chaos only, order shall emerge,
Unborn leaders shall be born,
Their utterances
Will be sharp as swords,
Cutting across the cross sections
Of hearts and souls
Making the minds free without fear.
For fifty long years

I am in self exile,
A self-imposed exile on myself.
It is a silent protest
Against decadence
Against degeneration
None bothered to understand,
Nor anyone cares for,
As 'let it be' is the golden rule.
I only know
What I am doing and why.
I know it is a world of imitators
And blind followers.
If you say 'yes'
You are optimistic,acceptable,
If you don't then
You are quickly branded
And isolated
As a potential scapegoat

■

THREE LINERS FROM SELF-EXILE

Fear of corona pandemic
Condemned all of us
To fight and win over it!

Days pass by in self-exile
My kith and kin are in quarantine
Death may press their door bell anytime.

I am moving between the cages of
My breathing room
And my living room endlessly.

My physical distancing
Has made me mentally distant
Hemming into my being and nothingness.

Hell is the other
Said existentialist Sartre
Corona pandemic only reminds that to us.

Roads are deserted
Is it a mourning symptom
For others and me too ?

Uncertainty, death and pandemic fear
Are all writ large on my face
Which I discover alone on my mirror.

Migrants are returning to their roots
But being potent carriers of killer virus
Their passage of return is only asymptotic.

Who can save the white ants
From a burning log,
Rootless fruitlessly returning to their roots!

I will not be there to display
The certificate of corona fighter
For claiming perks and allowances.

No need now to form human chain
For any cause whatsoever
Individual isolation rules.

Corona virus looms large on
All unions, associations, groups and trusts
Right of individual is in doldrums !

It is not a mere struggle
It is a fight to live for a day,
No other choice available for survival.

Outdoors corona contaminates physically
Indoors contagion films and data in media
No escape from its sinister presence.

In days of self-exile
Days dates months are so meaningless
Burn the calendar and the wall clock.

Unless you burn structures, records,
Calendars, clocks and hospital aprons
They may remind of the killer virus.

She has kept her shop open
But all her customers are hiding
It is a bad time for her flesh business.

I have no social identity
Except in so called social media
Even RIP is real in virtual domain!

Self-styled leaders too
Are in self-exile
Frantic to emerge from their cocoon.

Orphans are rootless, identity-less
Condemned to live in self exile always
Lockdown, unlock have no meaning for them.
My outlook has changed
Family members look like strangers
It is time for me to do their litmus test.

Rituals and practices have been condensed
It is time to relook at the prescriptions
In the holy scriptures and procedures.

Whether Hippocratic or Public oath
Taken once and forgotten to glory
For self-aggrandizement .

People are blind followers
Make them a herd like animals
They will follow you even to hell.

If you can cheat people repeatedly
If you can intoxicate them for a cause
You become a state not an individual.

None can hammer the last nail
Into the coffin of Corona.
It shall remain as a residue forever.

Life oscillates between birth and death
Transient equilibrium in between is poison
Some call it love, some devil.

Poison pollutes without discrimination
Poison kills without discrimination
Poison is where existence is.

Death is inevitable antithesis ,
Life is meaningful
So long there is death.

Life often appears as a reflection
On the mirror of death,
Or Is it a mirror image of death?

I was dying every night,
In the midst of death and death around
I was waking up to see myself alive

Like an idle ailing animal
I was eating and sleeping,
Waking up to eat and sleep again.

Masked son of the soil returns but dies
For no entry into the village
Village Goddess is also behind a mask

Unknown I came unknown I went
There was no need for a grave
Last remains were swept away by the flood.

They wanted to keep me in a mausoleum,
But the mortal relative burnt me till ashes
So that I fade away from the memory.

They were all make-shift warriors
Allured and assured for a false martyrdom
These cowards died in a pseudo-fight.

When they were made heroes overnight,
And even sang the patriotic song in chorus
Onlookers stood witness to a decadence.

As I dislike the jail and the hell
I have preferred to be a mute witness
Watching the country move to its own abyss.

The quest is all.
We are all seekers, none knows why
And it is an un-ended quest
Let there not be accuracy
As it kills poetry
Let there be labour of love only.

If a copier claims to be a poet
Kill him, as he has murdered
The truth expressed by someone else.

Burn the records, the books, the evidences
After all knowledge is mystical,
Why should truth needs documents.

What use are the repositories
Of grammatized structures
In mundane or virtual books ?

On contemplation I discovered
So many philosophical claims
Remain unclaimed even after centuries!

In quarantine they conserved
The fluid of love and tears
For the good and bad days ahead.

■

ORIFICE

Life long like a bee she stores sweetness
And like a silkworm
She weaves a cocoon of gossamer
And lives in it.
She perfumes all her orifices
Sharpens and polishes her nails
For her own pleasure.
Gossamer net is an extended product
Of the lubricant from her orifice,
And she always makes it perfect,
With her crafty skill of a spider.
Family , food, fun and funeral
All happen in the gossamer.
And one day
The gossamer is sucked
Back to the orifice,
And the silk worm too becomes extinct.
But the web of gossamer
Get created elsewhere
And it goes on ad infinitum.

CRIME & PUNISHMENT

Crime is committed
At the spur of a moment.
Fixing punishment takes time
Through the legal procedures.
Delayed punishment
Is no punishment.
The onlookers are restless
They know delay conceals
Bribe, nepotism, false-witnesses
Destroying documents and evidences.
Whether the instrument
Is a pen, a sword, an axe,
A firing squad or a hangers rope
Let it be used quickly
And of course judiciously.
Like eviction
Eviction must go on
Ands must be exhibited visually
For an indelible impact in the mind.
Lest the criminals shall mushroom
And rule the world.
Only the song of humanitarianism
Is not enough.
A populace, a state must
Reward and punish the deserving.

Summary disposal, Court martial
Shall tower over the of institutions
Of judiciary already in reds
Languishing under its own loads.
Let the instruments of execution
Be displayed in museums
Along with other dead artefacts
For the visitors to reminisce their
Obsolete history.

■

PERIODICITY

Nothing is known
Before the beginning
And beyond the end.
But from the beginning
Till the end
Everything is bound
By something or other.
There is a periodicity.
Periodicity is life
Periodicity is rhythm.
There is day and right
Week month and year.
Cosmos has its own periodicity
Of another dimension
The yin and yang
The female and male elements,
Have their own periodicity.
Women menstruate monthly
Vasundhara, the earth too
 Is believed to menstruate
When the rains shower on earth
Every year,
End of periodicity Is possibly the end of everything :
The apocalypse !

EARTH OF MORTALS.

I see him (Him) in you.
All the Time, every time.
He is dead they say
Therefore your waiting
Is for your last moment.
I appear charge
Everything around me
Also appear to change.
Nothing charges
Except at the precipice:
 Mortals cannot conceive
As to what happens there.

They can only see through
Their morbid glasses.
I too am mortal
I see you waiting for death
Like me and others
Before that happens
We have declared
Him dead.
How can he live scot free
On the earth of mortals ?
Immortals have no place on this earth
Immortals are man made

Created by groups
With vested interest.
No statue s immortal
It only reminds mortality
No work is immortal
In the frame of tome & space.

■

VISIT ENDS

When a man becomes a godman
When a man becomes a miracle man
When a man becomes a faith healer.
Many revere him as God .
Others label him as scoundrel.
The godman and the onlookers
Forget that they are mere visitors
To this earth.
In vain they claim
"I am my own successor ".
"Let my ashes be sprinkled
From high airs to the earth!'.
The seducer of souls
Offen die of pain and suffering
Like any other man in slum.
Let us not forget
This short visit has a beginning
And ending too .
Existence itself decides
Its own timing of a dissolution
Into infinite space and time.

■

SETTING SUN

I do not look at the setting sun
None bids farewell teeth dipping sun,
Everyone welcomes the rising sun
For its newness, bringing fortune!
Per chance when the sun sets
In front of me
With its penetrating blood rae rays
I remember my bygone ancestors.
With all the gory days agony
The sun dips slowly into the horizon.
To rise again as a new sun
On the other part of the globe.
Imaginary seven horses of the sun
Are abandoned daily ag the Sun

Are adorned daily
By the setting sun
At the undefined corner of
The Black pogoda,
The Konark (the solar corner) *
The dark shadow of the pagoda
Casts long lasting effect;
Sad, silent and spellbinding !
It is to be seen, to be beliewed

*A world heritage site in Odisha , India

A DESIRE I LIVE WITH

It is a desire I live with
It is a wish I know
Shall remain unfulfilled.
Still I shall live
With my little wishes.
I live my life,
Knowing well
That my and will be
A small urn of ashes
To be immersed
In the vast sea
By the kith and kin.
I know very well
There is no scope of choice
But given a chance I wish to die in daytime
In early winter
When the sky clear
And he says worm.
Let my bier carriers
And the onlookers
Get a good feel and warmth
Near the funeral flame
When the body gets burnt

■

GOOD BYE

It is time to say
Goodbye to you all
Forgive me
For all my misdeeds,
And all my
Pre-matured utterances.
Now I realize
It was all real
Life, sex, hunger food, war
Crime and punishment...
It was so unreal
Faith, religion, belief
Knowledge, argument...
All these now reappear
From my remote and recent memory
As a compact passing flashback.
I have now no regrets
For having lived such a life
Which I condemned while living it.

LIFE

When body does not support
Mind pretends to support
Living life beyond sixty is no life.
Showing off through public presence,
Attending spiritual discourses
Jogging, laughing a meditating
Is only a pseudo presence
Organic life is nothing but
A normal statistical distribution,
It rises to its own peak
And then falls slowly inevitably.
Peak is always like a needle tip
None can stay at apex for long.
Rise to reach the peak
And then fall from it is synonymous.
Rise only defines the fall.
No regrets
For everything done or not done.
It is time to leave the way
For the contenders,
It is time to give freedom to others,
Banyan tree shade of sixty years
Is fading fast
Saplings under its shade
Want to grow freely,

They are all belated & stunted
For lack of sunshine.
Let them grow to their own peak.
Living life beyond sixty is no life
It has prospered enough
It is time to perish
To linger or to expedite
Is no longer in our hands.
Unburden life if you can
To proceed on a luggage free journey
Towards the unknown.

■

GUN POINT

It was a near death experience
When I was in deep coma,
Diagnosed cerebral malaria
Parasites accumulated in brain !
Job, love, competition, punctuality
Duty, loyalty commitment, deadline
All reduced to nothingness
To exist, to survive against death
Was the only priority.
I fought alone
None else can fight proxying for me,
My parents prayed
And finally I won
Against all apprehensions that I won't
I returned as a bruised warrior
However, there was no welcome
 No bouquet of fresh flowers,
And I never hoped so.
I only saw a few tear drops
Falling from my mother's winkled eyes.
Today I live to give a floral welcome
To corona pandemic returned patients !
Returning from death
Has always been a new life to live
At gun-point!

■

THE LAST LICENCE

I realized late
That nature has blessed me
With a free licence
I wrote, I shaped pots and crafts
Invented ways to live and survive
When I look back I see
There were peaks of activities
And plateaus of inactivity too.
Still my licence was renewed
Nature was generous to me
Now I feel the validity
Is going to expire very soon
And may not be renewed further
As I too shall expire.
I know the licence
Has always an expiry date.
Even after I become invalid
The licence may for sometime remain valid
And then ceases to be meaningful
A gesture of gratitude of nature
To an ungrateful like me.
Like an ever pardoning mother
She thinks I have done my best !

A WISH

I desire to die on the same day
A leader is politically assassinated,
A leader who mechanised,
Computerised, digitised everything
Snatching the right of men to work.
Many starved without work
Their corpses were having depleted muscles.
As a writer unknown in the milieu
Nothing I did except writing.
Honest writing, no copying
Only describing truthfully
Are languishing as piles of paper
In my little house
Leaving no space for me to live,
In a system where mouth is stitched
Fingers are purchased
To remain inactive...
What can the winter do ?
Fungi have taken over
In the writers brain, nostrils
Armpits, genitals and anus.
He does not know
Whether he is alive or dead
I live a life of
Suspended animation,
Worse than death : ■

SPHINX

When the sphinx gurgles
It is ominous
When the sky gets molested
It is an ominous cyclone.
When the dog barks looking ahead
It is an evil spirit passing.
Rats come out from the holes,
Birds move erratically,
Indicate men the danger ahead.
There is an element of sphinx
In the nature,
In man and animals.
A sixth sense.
Sixth sense itself is sphinx
??d? of lion
And head of a man !
Sphinx warns against
The impending danger.

VISCERA

With a sharp knife
A quick slit I made
Into the viscera of India..
I never knew
Within her body
She has stored so much
For the seekers to see!
Gemstones, spirituality,
Threads to bind
Love to unite the mankind !
I am baffled by her
Hidden Treasure.
She is aboriginal,
She is beautiful
She is fulsome
She stands for a value
Which never withers.

MUTINIES

Mutinies do not occur.
Just like that
They are made to happen
In the minds of the people.
And then
It really happens In the physical world.
Values are auctioned
Beliefs are thrashed
And the mind crosses
It's own threshold.
There is revolt
There is rebellion.
There is mutiny
And finally death.

Death champions
The cause of mutiny
Death gives
The ornamental Certificate
Of history being made.

HOUSE ARREST

When one returns to his own self
There is house arrest.
Man's vocations, occupation
Shift him from his equilibrium.
There is a perpetual return
Back to his own self.
When man is in house arrest
Within himself ,
Contemplation, Knowing thyself
Meditation, Yoga
Become synonymous
To this house arrest.
It is nothing but self abandonment.

END GAME

I am the sword
Not the sword-holder
I am the flame
Not the smoke,
I am the sword
I am the flame.

I offend, operate
Never I defend nor maintain
I leave the scar on earth
I kill the good
I kill the bad
I destroy the big and the small.
Nothing survives before me
When I am on a spree

None can contain me.
Neither the law
Nor the women.
Nature shuns away from me.
Sun and moon hide as spent force
I trod on this sunless earth.
No trials, no tribulation.
I am the end-game.

DEATH

I pity death
A lonely existence.
Death is condemned
To be there as it is.
Everything goes into it
On as is where is basis,
Death levels everybody

I pity death
Because death cannot die
To understand love and life.
I pity death because
It defines life
Without becoming life !

Unless there is death
Love is meaningless
Life is cheerless.

■

SPIDER

I am the spider,
I have woven the gossamer;
I am responsible
For such creation around me.
It is a network
Of love-hate relationship.
Now, it is time to wind up.
I want to suck into myself
All that I have created.
I know, all those
Who have been trapped
Into my network,
Have reached
Their point of no return.
I do not want to leave
Any trace of my legacy.
Let everything and everybody
End with my own cessation.

NOW HERE NOW NOWHERE

Before you are a laughing stock
Before you become a patient of amnesia.
Finish your unfinished agenda
And prepare for your own exit.
Remember,
What you thought real all along.
Was your own make-belief;
What you ignored as unreal
Contains all your deeds and misdeeds
Fully encrypted for all times.
Everything every moment
Gets diluted invisibly
In infinitesimal proportions,
Into that universal sink.
After your mundane departure
Your existence becomes irreversible
But your utterances, thoughts, feelings
Come into the minds of men
Causing emotional turbulence
For reasons unproven.
That is perhaps the dynamics
Of your existence.

Therefore, prepare, get ready
Set yourself
And slip into the unknown
Without a flutter.

■

LAST WISH

I know very well
When I die
Nobody shall cry.
My body shall become
A raw bundle.
Of flesh & bone .
Before it smells like hell
It must be disposed off.
Wood and oil
Need not be wasted to burn.
No need to burn
A rootless man
On the lap of village ground,
Pristine village air
Need not be polluted.
Electric arc crematorium
Is enough and befitting
To convert me irreversibly
Into a handful
Of warm ashes !

BLACK EAGLE BOOKS

www.blackeaglebooks.org
info@blackeaglebooks.org

Black Eagle Books, an independent publisher, was founded as a nonprofit organization in April, 2019. It is our mission to connect and engage the Indian diaspora and the world at large with the best of works of world literature published on a collaborative platform, with special emphasis on foregrounding Contemporary Classics and New Writing.

www.ingramcontent.com/pod-product-compliance
Lightning Source LLC
Chambersburg PA
CBHW020540080526
44583CB00013B/923